dating
in the Age of
NARCISSISM

A SINGLE WOMAN'S SURVIVAL GUIDE

KIMBERLY MICHELLE

Palmetto Publishing Group, LLC
Charleston, SC

ISBN-13: 978-1-944313-21-0
ISBN-10: 1-944313-21-4

Asked by gossip columnist Hedda Hopper

how she knew so much about men:

"Baby, I went to night school."

-Mae West

Table of Contents

Introduction

Provehito in Altum

"Experience is the hardest kind of teacher.
It gives you the test first and
the lesson afterward."
—Oscar Wilde

M ost importantly, she remembers the pain. She remembers the friction of dry skin that tore and ripped to expose tender flesh. The very instrument that caused her so much pain and discomfort would one day become the focus of her affection. She was scorned for not being receptive to his "friend," scorned because her pre-pubescent body wouldn't open properly to receive his member. How could she be expected to sit on something, to allow it to enter her, when just a few moments prior, she wasn't even aware she had openings? She couldn't take the pain from any angle; she couldn't take it lying on her back, on her knees, or from behind.

The boy is now annoyed with her. Maybe he was frustrated that the opening of her vagina was no wider than a dime. Maybe he was upset at her because he couldn't cum, or because his dick was still hard and he knew that the girl he'd lured to this house was still standing behind him, her shadow cast to his left side.

What to do, he thought. He'd jerked off enough times to know a cure for blue balls. He knew this was going nowhere, because it wouldn't even go in all the way. He still had his back turned to her, all the while her shadow growing taller against the wall. She is standing behind him, watching his back and forth motions that appeared on the opposite wall. She pokes her head around to the left side of his body, but he then moved to the right.

"Open your hand," he said.

She does, and instantly he filled her hand with a warm, slimy substance. Afterward, he stood there in the dark and got dressed. Before he quickly exited through the window, he left her with one last sentiment.

"Next time, learn how to suck a dick."

With that, he was gone, and so was her virginity.

The next day, the whole school knew her name, but not by the one her mother had named her, but by the one *he* had given her. That little girl was me. I hadn't even had my first period yet. I felt the repercussions of my decision every day for my entire sixth grade year. I was teased, taunted, and called every bad name a person could be called. I acted out in class on purpose just so I wouldn't have to subject myself to all the bullying. I was kicked out of regular classes, and remitted to a single room with the other outcasts the school didn't want to deal with. I wasn't allowed to see the other kids who called me "whore" anymore, or see the boys who'd taken my glasses and run with them down the hall, giving other boys the opportunity to feel me up. I didn't have to avoid the snobby girls who didn't allow me in their circles because of my "whore" status. I could be with other kids nobody wanted around, and feel accepted. I felt love surrounded by losers. My confinement was my refuge.

My mother and father always had issues, and I'd never seen any real affection between the two of them. One particular day comes to mind. This day, like so many others I can't forget, are horrifying images, stuck like pieces of glass in my brain. There was no running water in our home or electricity. The water had been off for so long that the sewage began to creep up through the toilets and bathtubs, and eventually overflowed onto the carpet. I remember having to tip toe through the hall to my brother's room because of how saturated the carpet was with sewage. My brother's room was the only dry room in a house that smelled of feces and rust. He was a teenager, and was never home. Every day when I came home from school, I would take a large popcorn bowl and fill it with store-bought water to bathe. I sat naked, Indian-style on a towel in the middle of the floor, and took what old folks call a "hoe bath." It had been so long since I had taken a real shower or bathed in a tub, that when I did bathe at a friend's house, my skin never stopped peeling off when I dried off with the towel. I couldn't wipe enough. I was like a snake shedding its skin. Was I to be made new? Not for many years later would I realize how these events affected every decision I would ever make.

I can only say that I was once a normal little girl who watched Disney movies and wanted to be a real-life princess one day. I believed in magic and that enchanted feeling that Christmas time brings. At eleven years old, however, there was no one around to tell me that what I had given away for free in some shoddy vacant house, men would pay millions for. No one told me that what I had given away could never be recovered—not for all the money in the world.

The school contacted my grandmother. She didn't want to pull me out in the middle of the school year, so she had a church family keep me with their daughters. I'm not saying that my grandmother didn't love me. I know she surely did. I wanted to know then what I want to know now. Why isn't a child's love strong enough to beat addiction? Isn't love the most powerful weapon on earth? Or is that Disney bullshit? Little girls look for men to feel protected, to be made to feel safe. When there isn't anyone, around you take what you can get. Anyone will do.

I started to fight and lash out. I got arrested at thirteen years old for assault, trying to prove that light-skinned girls weren't weak. I had sex with anyone who was interested, smoked weed, and went to church with my grandmother on Sundays. She did her best with me. I played the piano, sang in the choir, and even got fingered through the large-sleeved gaps of choir robes as I sat next to older boys. Altos are the closet to the tenors, you know. I even continued this foul behavior in school, finding it thrilling that a hand was up my skirt during science class. You didn't have to ask me twice—you could get it the first time. I had become the very monster I'd been called a few years earlier—*slut.*

What is a slut? The urban dictionary describes it as a "woman with the morals of a man."

Merriam–Webster's Dictionary defines "slut" as a "slovenly or promiscuous woman." If you'll notice, these definitions mention nothing about men being capable of being sluts. So what exactly is a man called when he is slovenly or promiscuous? Oh, that's right; he's just being a man. Or he might be considered a whoremonger. But let's be real—the term "whoremonger" and/or "womanizer" has no real seriousness or negativity attached to it in the real world. Men are celebrated and even encouraged when they are whores and sluts, right from the time they have any understanding about it at all. Women are taught as soon as they're able to breathe to close their legs and keep their skirts down, not to have premarital sex, and to always be a lady. So if men are encouraged and women are discouraged, what sort of situation does that create? A three- tiered sexual caste system consisting of wives, whores, and men.

Which class do you belong to? Or have you decided to secretly straddle both sides of the fence? In my opinion, all women are both wives and whores, if the term "whore" has any real meaning. Words can't truly define a human being anyway. If you want to sleep with a hundred men, do it. Just protect yourself and don't tell anyone. Always, under every circumstance, lie and deny…unless there's a picture.

After my middle school and high school years, I tried hard to believe all that "good-girl-marriage" hype. I even got married as a way to cement my belief in marriage, and to calm my antiquated fears of going to hell for having premarital sex. It didn't last long, and we were soon divorced.

Things went on this way for years. I had steady boy-friends who always had my loyalty, but there was always that itch to seek more, and I always believed that the grass was greener and that I could find better. I've had some great men in my life, some of whom I've abused, and others who have abused me. I have failed more times than I have succeeded. I've had one husband, five marriage proposals, and countless boyfriends and lovers, but yet I am still single. Is this by choice? Yes. Yes, it is. I'm still optimistically waiting to cash in my golden Willy-Wonka ticket. I could be married right now to men who have loved me, who have wanted to set me up in the most luxurious of lifestyles, with money, cars, clothes, and status. I am a fool—the best kind of fool, though, because I love, love. I love the idea of *being in love*. I will take real love any day over diamonds and Gucci dresses.

I know exactly what it feels like to be taken care of by a man whom I don't love. The sparkle of new dresses, and freshly done hair and nails all wear off for me when I don't love him. It doesn't matter if I have not a bill to pay in the world because he's taken care of it all if I don't love him. As long as I don't love him, I will always be looking for an escape route. I used to have no problem sleeping with a man solely based on his status, wealth, or how I'd look on his arm at a party—who I could make jealous and envious just by being with him. I could con a man into thinking he was my sunrise and the sunset. The only problem was keeping up the charade.

I am writing this book because I am a serial dater, and I have failed and experienced so much in relationships with men that I now deem myself an expert. My advice always seems to work well when given to all my friends, but it never works for me. Does that sound familiar to you? You give the best advice but can't take it? As you read this, I hope you will consider me as one of your good girlfriends. I hope you will see all my failures and use them to find success. If you want marriage, a boyfriend, or just a lover, if you are a single woman, or even a single mother—this book is for you. Dating has never been more complex in the age of narcissism, yet some of the same old school rules still (unfortunately) apply. Women have jumped on the feminist progressive train, while most men are still trapped in a double-edged chauvinist mind frame; so if you want a man, you have to play his game, or at the very least you will need to think like a man until you can get what you want out of him.

part 1

the flags

Chapter 1

Red Flags

"We do not see things as they are,
we see them as we are."
—Anais Nin

Why is it that when you find someone you're interested in, everyone can find flaws except you? For example, to everyone else it's obvious that the dude is crazy or insane, but you just can't see it. Why? When we are in "like," lust, love, or when we're lonely, we become blind, deaf, and fucking stupid. Because we're women, we can't control ourselves. Everything goes back to some romantic comedy we saw, or even so far back as the story of Cinderella. I'm here to tell you: you are no princess. You have a better chance of winning the Texas lottery than you have of joining a royal family. It takes a mature woman to realize that no one is coming to save you.

Even if Prince Charming just happened to ride up on his mighty white steed, he's still not perfect, and neither are you. The only one that can save you is you. Men know just what to say to sleep with you. They play to what they KNOW we want, and they use it to their full advantage. Even the nice guys—the possibility of pussy is always a game changer.

Some things should be obvious to you. If you have to fight with your instincts over whether or not to date a guy, then that's a bad sign. It also indicates you don't think highly enough of yourself to do better, and that you'll make up any excuse as to why you should keep that dickhead around. These obvious signs are called *red flags*. When you notice something about a guy that doesn't seem right, your insides are constantly in a knot, or if you're afraid to speak up—these are red flags. Red flags can often be seen by everyone else in your life apart from you, so remember that. Let's break them down, shall we?

HE'S MARRIED, AND NOT TO YOU

This is the #1 red flag. You might say that this is an apparent red flag, and that you would never do such a thing, but millions of women are doing it every day, and have been doing it since marriage was invented. I've seen men go so far as to go through an entire party with their left hand in their pockets in order to hide their wedding rings. Never disrespect yourself or lower your value by dating a married man. Knowingly dating a married man increases your karma tenfold. What you do now will inevitably come back to you. It doesn't matter how much you like this guy, or how well you two mesh. If he's married, he's not the one. As much as you don't want to, think about the other woman involved in the situation. She's at home trying to be the perfect wife, while you sneak around with her man. We women are sisters, so think of her as such, and dump his ass—immediately. If he will do this to the woman he swore before God and family he would be faithful to, you can guarantee he'll do the same to you. You can bet money on it! Most cheating husbands are just looking for a new sexual adventure, because unlike women, they have no emotional attachment whatsoever when it comes to sex. Additionally, married cheaters usually have no ambitions to leave their wives. He just wants a quick roll in the hay, and then he wants to return home for supper.

If he did leave his wife for you, would you really want him? He's a piece of shit, and it won't be long until he starts stepping out on you too. It doesn't matter if he and his wife are living separately. They are still married. Just watch the news on any given week, and there will be at least one incident where a side piece was murdered by an enraged husband or wife. If you like him that much, wait until they are divorced. No exceptions.

Here are the top things that married men say:

- "We are separated."
- "I'm just staying for the kids."
- "She doesn't understand me like you do."
- "I wish I would have met you before I met her."
- "I don't love my wife like I love you."
- "We live in the same house, but don't sleep together."
- "She won't sign the divorce papers."
- "We haven't slept together in years."
- "I'm not attracted to her anymore."
- "I feel sorry for her."
- "We sleep in different rooms."

All of the above, of course, is complete bullshit, and, frankly, there aren't enough bullets to list the number of excuses out there.

NO PLACE TO STAY

He won't come right out and say that he has no place to stay. Instead, he'll make you think he wants to spend every waking moment with you. This will seem sweet, of course, because who doesn't want the man of her dreams to be with her 24/7? He'll slowly begin to bring in his toothbrush, work clothes, gym bag, extra shoes and you'll have to ask yourself, where would he be if he were not staying with me every night? Would he be on his mom's couch, or staying with his friends? Think about it. Isn't your place ideal? Not only does he get to sleep in the bed, he gets to sleep next to a hot chick, and that's not even taking into account any actual sex that goes on. You have air conditioning and cable, and you're gone during the day because of work. Also, if you're from the South, like me, you feed your man. It's like I stupidly carried them around in a basket, because I had this intense desire to take care of them.

Please don't do this—once or twice a week is fine, but you shouldn't make this a habit. You need your space too! This is your place. It doesn't matter if he's willing to pay rent. This is your place. Let a man be a man. Let him get his own place, and let him ask you to move in with him. Men shouldn't follow women. Don't feel sorry for him and think, *He can't get his own place right now.* You want a man that can pick himself up by the boot straps, make a way out of no way, and make something out of nothing. This is possibly your future husband. You don't want him being financially dependent on you. Your man should have just as much as you do, or preferable more than you do. If he is unemployed, he cannot live with you. Sometimes we get lonely, and that's okay, because *we all get lonely*. Letting an unemployed man stay with you, however, is never the answer. You will only hate him in the end, and you will hate yourself even more, because you knew better. Some of you want to be that "ride-or-die" or "down-for-my-man" type of chick, but listen to me when I say that that shit is for the birds. You will respect him more as a man if he can provide for himself. If you weren't there, what would his options be? He'd find somewhere to stay, for sure!

FOR SINGLE MOTHER

Unfortunately, when you decide to have children, you also decide to make some tough sacrifices. Remember, you are the first teacher from whom your child learns. No matter what your little one learns in school, it will be your actions and decisions that have the most profound effect on him or her. I've lived through all this shit, and I can tell you first hand—don't do it. Fatherless children are always looking to fill in the void. Once they see that you like this guy, and that he is staying over, they will begin to bond. Your little one will be so excited to spend time with this man, because there wasn't a man there before, and once he's gone, you won't be the only one with a broken heart. Your little one will hurt too. Never bring multiple men around your child. A male child will think this is how all women are, and will equate all men leaving as the natural order of life. Little girls, who want to be like mommy, will think that it's okay to be promiscuous. Don't bring a man around your kids for at least six to eight months, or until he has proposed; then, and only then, should you introduce him to your kids. Let the engagement period be the time where he gets to know them and if it doesn't work out, he'll have to move on. Any man who loves the mother, will do everything he can to love her children as his own. I know this sounds extreme, but you must be certain this man is serious about you and your kids. Does he want to be a stepfather? What do you expect from him as a stepfather? You have to think of your children's sanity, and know that they are silently watching your every decision and move.

Another rule to live by is that he is not allowed to stay the night around your kids. If this man can't even find a room of his own where you all can do your thing, then what do you need him for? I don't even recommend showing him pictures of your children. Some men date women to get to their kids. Pedophilia is real. Never leave a boyfriend to look after your children—never. There have been more cases than you can imagine where babies, young girls, and boys have been molested, raped, and killed by boyfriends to whom the mother entrusted her children. You will never forgive yourself if this happens. The world we live in promotes child pornography on a daily basis. Don't put your young, blossoming teenage girl in a position where she could get raped. Wait to get to know this man and his people first. As a mother, you have no job more important in this world than to keep your children safe.

NO CAR

You need to ask some questions, and not be too judgmental. There are some good men who don't have rides, but the most important thing is that you need to know why this is the case. He shouldn't be content with not having a car. Depending on what city you're living in, it might be economically feasible to not have a car. In New York, it is easier to get on the subway than it is to actually get in a car, wait in traffic, and drive to wherever you're going. This is understandable. If you live in a metropolis, however, like Houston, where things are spaced out, it makes far more sense to own a car than it does to ride a bus. He needs to have a car.

If you get into a relationship with a man who doesn't have a car, you need to understand that you will be the one picking *him* up, and not the other way around. When I dated guys who didn't have cars, guess who was there any time they needed a lift? Me. I thought that I was showing him how much I could be there for him in his time of need, and this would make him keep me around, because I supported him while his was down. What a load of shit! I didn't ask a single question as to why a grown man didn't have a car, and when I did ask questions, all I got were lies. One guy told me he'd leant his car to a friend. Why would you leave yourself stuck in a position like that? If he doesn't have a car, the reason could be that his license is suspended, which means he might have a criminal record. If he works twenty-four hours a day, seven days a week, and still has no car, that can mean many things:

1. He's content not buying a car or saving money, so as long as he has access to yours.
2. He has a criminal record, or his license is suspended, in which case, you need to ask why.
3. He owes too much in child support, and simply can't afford it. It's up to you to decide whether you want to date a man that can't make enough money to support his children or himself.

You don't need a man that needs your help. He should be helping you. If you're convinced that who you're dealing with is truly a good man, let him take the bus to see you. If he is serious about you, those long bus trips will eventually start to annoy him. He'll get his shit together, and he'll get a car if it means losing you. Don't make arrangements that involve him taking the bus there and you bringing him back. Let a man be a man. You can

11

never respect your man if he is always in a needy, pitiful situation. I mean it when I say, don't you dare pick his ass up! I found out my car-less ex-boyfriend was using my car to pick up women to take out on dates. He even went so far as to move my baby's car seat and put it in the trunk to make it seem like it was his ride. Don't get used!

UNEMPLOYED

This goes without saying, ladies. If he doesn't have a job, he has no business dating you. You can remain friends, but it shouldn't go any further than that until he begins to show you he's serious about being in a relationship with you. You need a man who is employed. If he isn't employed, ask him why. Does he have a criminal record? If so, what did he do? Remember, if he isn't handicapped, any reason he gives you for not having a job is an excuse. If you decide to seriously date a man that is unemployed, know that you'll be the bread winner. A woman cannot respect a man whom she has to take care of. I don't care how attractive he is. Once you begin to see that he brings nothing to the table, all of his attractiveness will fly out the window.

If he says he owns his own business, check it out. Don't just take his word for it. Research his business. Does it have a website? Does he have employees? Can he support himself with this business? How long has he had this business? Is it legit? Remember, an unemployed man, will say *anything* to get inside your pants. If he can't talk about what type of business he's in, run! Stay away from "street pharmacists" and guys who deal in the sex industry. An unproductive man is not a provider. He's a loser. It's not your job to help him find a job, or introduce him to a new way of life because you see his "potential." You are not his wife. Know the difference. A man will always do what he wants to do. It is an excuse if he tells you he can't work due to a criminal history. He just doesn't want to work. Any job is better than no job. If he feels that it's better to live off a woman than it is to be a dishwasher at IHOP, then he is no man. Get rid of his ass!

CHILDREN BY MULTIPLE MOTHERS

Before I had a child of my own, I was very arrogant. I didn't believe a man would treat me the same way he treated other women. I thought I was different. Some of you may think you are different too, because of what a man has promised you. Let me tell you this—a man who has multiple children by different women is reckless. He doesn't use condoms, and he thinks that it's okay to make children with every woman he meets. The man I like to call my daughter's "sperm donor" had two children when

I met him. He barely took care of these children, and the mothers were always around, and they weren't happy. When I got pregnant, I never saw him again. I wish I'd understood that if he'd done it to them, he was going to do it to me, and the same holds true for you. There are some men who take care of all their children, but this is an exception. The reality is that even if he's financially taking care of all of his kids, they are still missing a father at home, which is something a check just can't replace. Did he marry any of these women?

Dating a man with multiple children means you will have to deal with multiple women, each of whom has an individual personality. Not all of those women will be understanding or sweet. Some will be downright disrespectful because of their anger toward him. Don't judge these women too harshly. If you don't leave now, you'll become just like them, a jilted, bitter baby mama. Do you really want to deal with this? No man is worth your sanity, sister—keep it moving!

CRIMINAL HISTORY

What I like to do when I want to get to know a man, is stalk his social media sites—Facebook, Twitter, Instagram, etc.—any social media account he has is a friend of mine. You'd be surprised how much you can learn by simply looking at his online accounts. If he has pictures of guns, drugs, and strippers surrounding him, then, believe me, that's what he's about. You are looking for a man, not a thug, and not a criminal. Look at the people who are tagged in his photos. What kind of people are they? Is their timeline also flooded with drug paraphernalia, strip club life, and violence in general? You are who you associate with, like it or not. Search for him on the FBI's Most Wanted list, search through public records, and through the United States Department of Justice's National Sex Offenders list. I know this may sound crazy to you, but the truth is that even a man you think you know has secrets. This may seem like a lot of work, but your life is on the line here. Women are murdered, and even worse, never found again, nearly every single day, often because they didn't take the necessary precautions. Do you know him to be quick tempered, to have a short fuse? Is he easily upset? How does he speak of women in his past? Does he speak about them with anger? Has he admitted to being, or do you know him to be, violent or physically abusive with women? Has he gone to jail for sleeping with a minor? Don't make excuses for bad behavior simply because you want a man. Life is short, so do your research. Never let him know that you checked up on him, however—never.

FOR THE SINGLE MOTHER

Not to diminish the responsibilities of your average single woman, but the single mother has far greater responsibilities, because she not only has to look after her own life, but she must look after her children's as well. You mustn't let a criminal around your children. However, know that you can't judge books by their covers, such as thinking of a man with tattoos as not being professional. For example, my brother spent thirteen years of his life in prison. He went in at eighteen years old, and didn't come out till his thirties. When he came home, his whole life revolved around making up for lost time, repairing the damage that occurred due to him being away, and generally starting anew. He married, had children, bought a house, opened his own business, and is about to finish college. He also works for a major newspaper that saw beyond his record, wanted to employ him for his intelligence, and admired his gumption.

He is the prototype for prison rehabilitation—the exception, however—and this rarity is one that occurs only about ten percent of the time. Please don't get caught up in thinking your man is the exception. This type of man knows he has to prove himself more than any other man because of his record. Watch him closely and take things at the pace of a snail, if possible. He should be a shadow of the man he was before. He must completely change, and it mustn't be an act. If it feels wrong to you, it is wrong. Trust your gut. God gave men physical strength, but he gave us instinct. Never second guess your gut. If the guy who supposedly wants to date you is still "'bout that life," leave him to it. He will be no good for you *or* your children.

MULTIPLE MARRIAGES

Being married multiple times is not as bad as it seems. At least the guy isn't afraid of marriage like many of his brethren, but this is a red flag too, of course. Why does he keep getting divorced? Is he the clingy type that just doesn't want to be alone? What are the real reasons he can't keep a woman? If he claims he was the victim each time, then you know something is up. There are three sides to every story—his side, her side, and the truth. Tread lightly where this is the case. There's likely a deeper issue going on here.

DEAD BEAT DADS VS. FATHERS OF THE YEAR

Never date a dead beat dad. The father is just as much responsible for the child as the mother. If he claims the mother won't allow him to see the child, ask him why hasn't he taken the necessary legal steps to enforce his parental rights. If he says he's not even sure if the child is his, ask him why he hasn't had a paternity test. Is he afraid the test will be positive, and he'll be responsible for child support? What about the child who's at the center of all this? You should desire a man of honor. If he slept with this woman, he should be doing everything in his power to find out if the child is his or not, *at the very least*. He must assume some of the responsibility if he slept with her. If he has a child he doesn't take care of, he is not a man.

If you see him being bashed on social media for being a loser father, then it's probably the truth. If you are a young woman in your twenties, don't even waste your time with this type of drama. There are plenty of men who don't have these issues and/or don't even have kids yet. Your dating pool is enormous when you're fresh out of college, and you'll probably still have luck in the clubs. As you'll find out in your thirties and forties, however, you start to notice that it's almost impossible to avoid dating a man who doesn't have children. When that's the case, you have to figure out if it's a situation you're willing to work through. Always ask yourself, is it worth it? Most of the time it isn't worth it, so just keep swimming. A father should make every effort to see his children, and this might mean excluding you a lot of the time. Unlike single mothers, who usually have full custody, a fathers time to see his children is often relegated to weekends only. That said, if he's a good dad, that's when he'll see them. Understand that this is how a good man behaves. You might not be able to date this type of guy, however, because even though he's a great dad, this means he might be a bad boyfriend. Don't be selfish. Don't make him choose you over them, or vice versa. You wouldn't want a man that would choose a woman over his kids. Is that how you would want your kids to be treated? Ask him directly what he wants from you. Work out a schedule that doesn't take time away from his kids. Schedule lunches throughout the work week, walks in the park, or movie dates. It can work, and when he is ready to bring you around his children, he will. Don't press the issue.

HE HATES HIS MOTHER

Little boys think of their mothers as the epitome of womanhood. He will treat you as well as he treats his mother. She can do no wrong, and your cooking will never be as good as hers, even if you are a chef. She is what every woman should strive to be. This is the first woman who knew his heart, and the only woman who will ever truly have it, no matter what. In his eyes, she is perfect. When a man is abandoned by his mother, rejected, or has witnessed her committing heinous acts, such as continually bringing different men around, their views on what they think about women become misconstrued. He can sometimes turn into a man who doesn't truly value women and/or mothers. If he curses at his mother, calls her a bitch, or never speaks to her when she calls, ask him why. He might even be following the example of an abusive father. You need to know to get the explanation required in order to excuse this type of behavior. A man that can speak to his mother so disrespectfully is not the man you need in your life. A man that has no respect for women is not the man for you.

OBVIOUS RED FLAGS

- Initiates sex on the first date
- Drug user
- Has no spirituality or religion in his life
- Makes negative references or comments about your weight ("You aren't normally my type.")
- Refuses to take no for an answer
- Refuses to wear condoms
- Quick to anger
- Has children under the age of two
- Narcissistic
- Wants to sleep with you, but insists on a friends-with-benefits scenario

- Calls you a bitch, slut, or a hoe (under no circumstances should you ever allow anyone to call you these things, joking or otherwise; there's nothing funny about being disrespected)

Chapter 2

Yellow Flags

---

*"Distrust and caution are the parents
of security."* —*Benjamin Franklin*

Some flags aren't as obvious as others. I'm going to use yellow flags as a means of indicating caution, i.e. these flags mean you should slow down and analyze the situation. When you are driving and come to a red light, you stop. When you see it's yellow, you might slow down, but you might keep going. Green, of course, means go! Yellow flags don't necessarily mean you have to instantly break up with someone. Yellow flags indicate issues that can be worked on, as long as both parties are in agreement—it's not just the female screaming ultimatums.

Yellow flags can indicate a deeper issue, one you may haven't been able to unearth yet. Yellow flags are good detectors for figuring out whether a man is interested in you or not. A yellow flag can make or break a relationship, and is often an indicator of whether or not we can proceed to the next stage, the stage where there are plenty of "green flags", which, of course, means you've made it to the winner's circle. You'll figure out who you're really dealing with during the yellow flags stage. At this stage, you shouldn't be sleeping together either. If you both have made it this far without being physical and his affections start to change, then you know why. He was just in it to win it, and he'll likely get out of it because you wouldn't give it up. If he's there to really get to know you, he'll be happy to just be in your presence. If yellow flags such as this aren't improved—and I mean soon—then a break up is not far away.

HE'S ALWAYS IN THE CLUBS

This is something that can change for him if he feels he's found what he's looking for. Going to the clubs is usually a pastime for young single men who are still on the prowl, and only interested in one night stands. I have never in all my dating life been in a serious relationship with a man who I met at a club. Older men use the outing as a getaway; it's not done often, but he will still go. If his college mate is celebrating turning forty, or his male family member needs a drink, he'll go. A truly committed and content man won't want to be out at the clubs every weekend. He'd rather be with you. Don't be a nag about it. If the man hasn't been out with his boys all month, let him go. Encourage him to go. Every person needs his or her space.

STRIP CLUB VIP

All women have their insecurities, and the last thing you need is your man frequenting a titty bar. I don't care how beautiful you are; you will eventually become annoyed if he goes to a strip club too often. What about those times when you're not sure if he's actually going to the strip club? If it bothers you, tell him it bothers you. If you want him to stop going, tell him. If he doesn't stop, then you need to stop seeing him. It's not about him doing what he's been doing before you all met. It's about him acknowledging your feelings. If he wants to keep you around and keep you happy, then he'll stop.

FEAR OF COMMITMENT

It doesn't take a man long to know what he wants. If you've been dating a year or two, and marriage hasn't even come up, it's time to talk. What are his plans for you in his future? You have a life to lead, and honey, it is *short*. Why isn't he ready? Are you ready? If you are okay with not being married, then that's okay too. Just make sure you voice that to him when you first start dating. Everyone has their reasons. Just so long as you are on the same page, you'll ensure things don't get messy in the end. You definitely need to know why he isn't willing to get married, however. Maybe he doesn't think you're the one.

Some men feel they don't have to marry if they're already being given everything they want. You act like a wife, but you're just his girlfriend. You treat him like a husband, but he's just your boyfriend. You cook his food, wash his clothes, fulfill him sexually, do favors for his family, pay bills together, maybe even invest in property together, etc., but you are *still* just a girlfriend. You're given all the duties of a queen, but you aren't allowed to wear the crown. It's in a glass box locked away. You are not allowed to touch it, but you can Windex the hell out of the case to keep it shiny.

Don't treat a boyfriend like a husband. As the old saying goes, "Why buy the cow, when you can get the milk for free?" My father used to always say this to me, and I never really quite grasped what that meant. Men are hunters. Men love to chase after something they can't have. Think of those English hunting scenes from Downton Abbey, or any hunting scenario you can imagine.

Think about how much work and preparation is put into getting ready for the hunt.

Everyone is excited because they don't know if they'll be successful or not, if they'll come back with a fat duck or a scrawny pigeon. As they begin to stalk their prey, their momentum builds as they go out deeper into the woods. They shoot, they miss, they shoot, they miss, they shoot, and then they hit their target! The hunter brings in what he's killed, and he's proud of it! He boastfully shows everyone his accomplishment.

Now think of the hunter not having to prepare for the hunt. He doesn't have to suit up, he doesn't need his dogs, and he doesn't even need a gun. The hunter sits down in his night robe at the dinner table, yawning. The venison is brought to him on a silver platter. He sighs, and eats everything in front of him. He's bored. There was no challenge. Everything was given to him easily. He has had to work for nothing.

My point, ladies, is to keep him excited and interested. Whatever you give him easily, he is bound to not appreciate. If you make him work for his "supper," he will value it all the more. It will be something he is proud of. How many men do you know who bring home a one night stand to meet their mothers? If you give him everything he wants, he'll say, "Why mess up a good thing with marriage? Everything's perfect now as it is." Yes, it is perfect—perfect for him, and you're in a perfectly un-committed relationship.

HE WON'T INTRODUCE YOU TO FAMILY OR FRIENDS

I once dated a guy who I thought was really serious about me. When I would come through the door, along with my daughter, he would hurry to get off the phone with his mom. Jokingly, I asked if he was trying to hide us from his parents. He slipped up, and said that he didn't want his mom to know he was staying with "some chick." He quickly corrected himself, but that was all I needed. I remember telling him I thought this was a red flag, that I wasn't just "some chick," and that my daughter and I were real, that we existed. Yes, I am overly dramatic.

He then began to tell me that he didn't mean it that way, that his parents were really religious, and that they could be very judgmental. This guy was forty-three years old, and he was still worried about what his parents thought. Yeah, right. I told him that what he was saying was bullshit, that it seemed like he was trying to hide us, and that he wasn't taking our relationship seriously. A few weeks passed, and I began to ask about why I hadn't met any of his friends. He said he "wasn't ready for that yet." More bullshit. We had been dating for four months, we lived together, and he had met almost everyone in my family. I finally argued with him about it, and put him out of the house. I made several mistakes in that relationship, one of which was simply moving too fast. First of all, never live with a guy after only seeing him for four months.

If you are both dating each other exclusively and you haven't met anyone he knows after a month or two, something is up. When a man loves you and wants to be with you, he's proud of you and wants to show you off. He wants to let all his friends and family see what a beautiful woman he has at his side. He wants people to be impressed. If he hides your relationship, or if you even have to ask, you need to end it. He doesn't really want you. In my case, he just needed a place to stay, a meal, and free pussy. Some women don't realize this, and they go on for years in a relationship having never met anyone their guy knows. Sadly, eventually they come to realize the reason why.

HE TALKS ABOUT SEX ON THE FIRST DATE

I consider this to be both a red and yellow flag. If you are desperate, lonely, or horny, this will come off as a compliment. It's not a compliment. He is trying to fuck you, and he thinks you owe it to him because of the money he's putting out for the date you're on. What do you want from him? Do you just want sex? Or do you want a relationship? If you want a relationship and all he talks about is sex (he asks you if you like being spanked, for instance), end the date. At the very least, finish the date with your belly full, and never answer any of his calls again. You know what he is about. It's not cute that he's known you for less than twenty-four hours and is already talking about sexual positions. It should be a major turn off for you, because it *is* a turn off. This kind of guy is looking to score, has no other type of conversation, and is usually an egomaniac. Move on!

LET'S CHILL

I totally get that paying for two people to eat and go to a movie or a play is expensive. I understand that. But don't be fooled. A man who is interested in you will not have you to his home on the first date, or even the second date. He will try his best to wine and dine you. If he can't afford that, he will find something for you all to do—but it won't be "Netflix and chill." "Chill" is code word for cheap, and even worse, fucking. Don't be a cheap lay. Let him know that you're looking for something serious, and that you don't know him like that to be all up in his house that soon. This isn't high school—you are a grown woman looking for a grown man.

Besides, no woman wants to be with a cheap man. You want to be with a man of means. If he can't afford to date, then he shouldn't be asking you out until he's financially secure. If you are both college students, this might not be possible to achieve yet, as you both might be poor and living on ramen noodles. Nevertheless, have some dignity, and he'll respect you more in the long run, and his respect is ultimately what you want. If this guy is poor, and he really wants to be with you, nothing will stop his creative juices from flowing. He will *find* a way to woo you—with or without Ramen noodles.

NEVER CALLS, ALWAYS TEXTS

Technology has ruined us. It has taken away the awkward interaction between human beings that's needed in order to form connections. Nothing is real anymore. I need to hear you panting and stuttering on the phone when you call me. I need to hear the quiver of your voice because you are excited to be speaking to me. I want to hear you laugh out loud! I don't want to read "lol." How many of us type "lol" and haven't even cracked a smile? Texting takes away the spirit of a conversation. I can't tell if someone is mad, sad, facetious, or comical unless they leave me a fucking emoji at the end of every sentence! Insist that a guy you meet online calls you first before your text relationship begins. Have long conversations; make it a rule to only text if you can't talk at that time—whether you're at work, driving, or on the can. Be a human again. There's nothing better than having a man who you're into call you up and ask you out. Fuck that texting shit. Anyone can do that. Not only is it the right thing to do, it is the most romantic thing to do. Insist on being treated like a lady at all times.

STUCK TO HIS PHONE

I hate to be asked a question, and then the person who asked it looks down at their phone to check their Twitter or Facebook. It's even worse when that person laughs at whatever they've just seen on their timeline—all while claiming to listen to your answer. This guy is not interested in you. He's just killing time until what he really wants comes along. You're just there taking up space, filling a void, all while he hopes you'll give up some pussy. This guy has many women, which is probably why he never leaves his phone around you. He has a code, and he makes sure to enter it fast. Remember, he's an idiot— so his code is probably his birthday, his college football number, or the birthday of one of his kids. When he's sleeping, showering, or even taking a shit, he never lets that phone too far out of his reach. Yet when you call him, he never seems to pick up, claiming he left his phone in the car, or the battery died—for the whole night. Then when he's with you, it's always charged or charging. If he has a call he doesn't want you to hear him answer, he either sends the caller to voicemail or runs outside like a thief. *He's always texting and receiving texts.* That's my point. He'll tell you it's his boys, work, or a family member. If there is someone who is calling or texting repeatedly, he'll say it's a family member he's quarreled with, and doesn't want to take the call. If you do see an unknown woman in his phone, he might tell you it's his homie's girlfriend looking for him. He'll say anything but the truth. When he loses it, he panics. He can never go without his phone. He has secrets, lots of them, and it'll only be a matter of time before you find out what they are.

REFUSES TO OPEN DOORS, PULL OUT CHAIRS, OR PAY FOR MEALS

If you've been around the block, no one knows that fact except you. He has no idea of your past; therefore, he should always treat you like a lady unless at some point you show him otherwise. I am a black woman; I usually date black men. On one date, with a black man, we approached the doors to the restaurant, and my date just stood there behind me. I was confused, and there was an awkward silence between us. I said, "Aren't you going to get the door?" He furrowed his brow, and he said, "Oh, I guess you think you some kind of white girl, don't you?"—as if being a black woman meant I didn't deserve the same amount of respect as a white woman.

Never let any man treat you like you don't deserve respect, simply because you might not look like a plastic Barbie doll. If you are overweight, short, black, white, Latina, Asian, a foreigner, have a limited education, no matter what—you are still a woman, and a man who requests your time should be kissing your ass. You are the prize, and he asked you out; you didn't ask him. Pulling out chairs is something young guys rarely do. Not because they are disrespectful, but because they simply don't know. An older man will pull out your chair, and he won't even allow you to get out of the car on your own. He will come around to open the door and get you. Not all men are like this, old or young alike. But if you do find a man who does these things, keep him on your "yes" list.

If you have a nice guy who doesn't do these things, let him know that you love being treated like a lady, and that you would appreciate it if he would do these things for you. Ask sweetly, and never demand. If he really wants to please you, he'll enjoy making you happy. If a man doesn't pay for your meal on a date, he is a loser. Never see this jerk again. No questions asked. He asked you out! He pays for the meal. If you are seriously dating, then it doesn't hurt to pick up the tab every now and then to let him know you appreciate him, but do not make it a habit. Real men do not like a woman taking care of them. Only a bitch will sit back and let you pay for everything all the time.

PLAYS MISOGYNISTIC MUSIC AROUND YOU

First impressions are everything. He doesn't know you. All he should assume is that you are a lady. If you get in his car and the music blaring includes lyrics like, "Bitches ain't shit but hoes and tricks," he isn't used to dealing with grown adult women. He's used to messing with trash. Set him straight quick. If he would feel uncomfortable playing this disrespectful music around his mom, sister, or grandmother, he should feel awkward playing it around you too. You are to be respected, and men will treat you like you *let* them treat you. We woman are what we say we are. Words can be powerful, because words, do, in fact, have meaning. Are you actually a four-legged female dog? Are you actually a whore? Remember, you are the stage director and you set the scene for how this script will play out. Besides, a grown, mature, sexy man is what you want, someone who knows what the power of a smooth love ballad can do to a woman's heart. A man who has an appreciation for good, quality music is a man of taste and class. Don't get caught up in what's popular. Know the difference between taste and trash.

WHO ARE HIS FRIENDS?

I hate clichés, and for that reason I will not use them. But there is truth in clichés. We are who we hang with. Are all his friends single? Or are they all a bunch of bitter divorcees, out there playing the field? If all his friends are married, and he is the only single one, this is a good sign. If all his friends are hoes, hitting up the clubs three times a week, then he probably is too. Birds of a feather...dammit! I said I wouldn't use clichés. but you get the idea I hope.

TOO MANY FEMALE FRIENDS

There's nothing wrong with him having a female friend, but know their history. Have they slept together? Were they in a previous relationship? If he wants to be with you, he will not disrespect you if you feel uncomfortable about their relationship. If this female friend is a mature lady she'll understand that he has a girlfriend now, and that the nature of their relationship has to change. If all his friends are women, that will ultimately be a problem for you in a relationship. I am territorial, and I do not like women, friends, or not being able to spend enough time with my man. If she isn't his relative, then I have a problem with it. Talking on the phone and catching up is cool, but hanging out is a no-no for me. I mean, why is it necessary? Doesn't she have any girlfriends? What are her motives? Keep in mind too, that all great relationships start off as friendships. She might be trying to usurp your throne.

Here's a true story—my boyfriend had a ton of female friends. They would even camp out at his place from time to time. I'd come through the door, and there they'd be, sleeping on his couch or laying on the floor. I was so uncomfortable, not to mention, pissed off! Did I mention these women were strippers and prostitutes? Not to judge, but damn, I don't want them around my man! I don't care how long they've been friends. That's when I started to realize that I was dealing with a truly sleazy guy. He wouldn't turn those whores away for the world. Yet the very mention of a male friend of mine that he'd never met sent him into such a jealous frenzy I thought his head would pop off. Therein lies the proverbial double standard. Men can't stand the idea of you having male friends, because they know men. But we know women too, right? I was being so disrespected, and

I didn't even realize it. At one point I actually felt myself competing with them to get his attention. If she is a true friend of his, he will have no problem introducing you to her. You will feel comfortable, and not insecure about their relationship. She might even turn into your friend as well.

NO AMBITION

A man with no ambition is like a car with no engine. He is just sitting there. He doesn't want much, and is content with being mediocre. But don't judge him too harshly. Not every man you meet will have goals and ambition. Some men are happy to work eight to five for fifty years and retire with a gold watch. Some people are happy with a simple life, and that's okay. Just make sure that you are the same type of person. If you are an ambitious woman with big dreams and goals, and are acting on those goals every day, you should attract someone with that same type of spirit. If you are doing nothing, you will attract a man who is also doing nothing. Remember this is the man you might marry and have children with. What type of life do you want? And what type of man do you want? Don't think you can change him into being motivated. He should already know what he wants out of life. It is not your job to make him want a life. He has to want it for himself.

ADDITIONAL YELLOW FLAGS

- He wants to be a rapper at forty years old.
- He doesn't include you in his outings—ever.
- He doesn't wear condoms.
- He's addicted to porn.

Chapter 3

Green Flags
(The Frog Prince)

"To you I shall say, as I have often said before, don't be in a hurry, the right man will come at last."
—Jane Austen

Hallelujah! Finally, the blessed green flags! This is what you've been waiting for, to meet a man that exhibits all of the following fantastic qualities. If you meet a guy like this, then you have been doing all the right things. He is a rare commodity, and he knows it. Green flags stand out, but they can also turn an immature woman off. Be aware. If you have a man presenting green flags to you, and you find him boring, unattractive, or you are simply not that interested, check yourself—and quick!! Take a second look at this man. The best man for you is probably not the most attractive man in the room. Don't be rude to him. Hear him out, and don't you dare write him off. There are millions of single woman desperate to get their hands on Quasimodo.

Believe me, once you find out how great of a guy he is, he will turn into the man of your dreams. Your friends and family will not understand at first. Once they see that he treats you like a queen, they'll understand soon enough. Only a mature woman can give a not-so-handsome man a chance. A grown woman measures a man by how well he treats her and her children. She judges him by his actions and his heart. Everything that is beautiful today, will be dying tomorrow. You are looking for a life partner, not a Ken doll. Always be smart, however, because a good, seemingly perfect man can be a psycho too. Always do your research.

CALLS AND ASKS YOU OUT (NOT VIA TEXT)

Yes! An adult male with balls! He actually picked up the phone and asked you out. Score one for team green! This is such a rare occurrence nowadays, that it might not even happen to you. Even a good guy has become adjusted to the lack of chivalry currently present in our society, so if he does pick up that phone, he's something special.

PICKS YOU UP AND OPENS DOORS

I know you might be thinking that you would never go out with a man who didn't pick you up for a date or open doors for you. You know better than that, right? You wouldn't believe how many women regularly cater to men, picking them up for dates, opening their doors, paying for all the meals, and even getting down on one knee and proposing. Don't tell me you haven't seen this bullshit on social media. That said, it seems I must mention this here for the smart ass women who do dumb shit. He is supposed to open the door for you. You are a lady. He is supposed to pick *you* up for the date. If you don't feel comfortable with him knowing where you live, then meet him somewhere, but never pick up a man to take you out.

HAS HIS OWN CAR

Not his mama's car, baby mama's car or his cousin's car, but he has his own car. Again, you are not responsible for how he gets around town or for how he gets to work.

HAS HIS OWN HOME OR APARTMENT

Grown men shouldn't live with their mothers unless they are taking care of them. Lots of losers say they are taking care of their aging parents, and this is not true. They just know they don't have to pay tons of bills so long as their parents do. This guy is not necessarily a bad guy; he could be going through a divorce and may have lost everything, and is trying to rebuild his life. He might be going through some financial issues. In any case, this should be a temporary arrangement.

P.S. Don't let a grown man sneak you into his mama's house for sex. Grow up.

HE IS EMPLOYED

I will say that it shouldn't matter what a man does so long as he has a job and isn't depending on you for his next meal. But it does. Yes, he is employed, and that's awesome. Now what exactly does he do for employment? Ask yourself, is his job honorable? Can you tell people what he does for work and not have to lie or become embarrassed? Are you proud of him and what he does? Can this job provide for you and the future family you might build?

HE IS IN SCHOOL

This guy has a good head on his shoulders. He *wants* more than what he has. He *wants* to be a better man. He *wants* to be a man that can take care of his family. He *wants* you to be proud of him. Encourage him to study, and motivate him to finish. Let him know how proud of him you are, and how sexy you think it is that he is getting his degree.

HE TAKES CARE OF (ALL) HIS CHILDREN

No man is perfect. But if a man does everything he can to spend time with his child and tries his best to respect the mother—even if she is being crazy—he is a good man. This man will listen to a crazy woman rant, just so he can see his kid, and he won't curse her out. Be patient with him, and only offer advice if he asks for it. Don't stick your nose in his business.

ADDITIONAL GREEN FLAGS

- He has hobbies or motivations outside of work.
- He has ambition and wants greater things from life.
- He loves his mother, grandmother, sisters, aunts, etc.—he reveres all female members of his family and will not allow them to be disrespected.
- You've never heard him call a woman a derogatory word in anger.
- He is patient, kind, and respectful towards the elderly.
- He wants to introduce you to family and friends a few weeks into dating.
- Ninety percent of his friends are married or in long-term relationships.
- His friends are professional men, like him. He doesn't hang with thugs or wannabe thugs.
- He is religious or spiritual, and invites you to partake in said religion or spiritual practices.
- He compliments you on your appearance, and thinks you are perfect the way you are.
- You can depend on him if you are in need.
- He doesn't pressure you for sex, and is willing to wait until you are ready.
- He is not dating other women.
- He sends or brings you small gifts to let you know he is thinking of you.

- He asks you about yourself and your children.
- He is not a drug user.
- He includes your kids in activities that are age appropriate.
- He doesn't harp on the past or continually mention ex-girlfriends.
- He will protect you, and won't allow anyone to disrespect you.

part 2

---

the don'ts
& the dos

Chapter 4

The Don'ts

"I am only responsible for my own heart, you offered yours up for the smashing, my darling. Only a fool would give out such a vital organ."
—Anais Nin

This is a hefty chapter. We live in a topsy-turvy world were men act like women, and women act like men. Most of us are children of divorced or single parents, and we have seen first-hand abusive relationships as children. That means we don't necessarily know what to do, or what is right and what is wrong when it comes to relationships. There are a lot of don'ts here—I know— but if you read these next two chapters repeatedly, they'll begin to make sense, and these words will get stuck in your head. You want to remember what *not* to accept. You, as a lady, have boundaries. You can't let a man do any and everything to you, because they will. Men love to take advantage of weak women, because the pussy is free. They don't have to work for a weak woman. They will use her up until she's dry, and then go marry another woman the following week.

What kind of woman are you? I wrote this chapter of don'ts based on the numerous relationships I've been in, so I am not writing this from the standpoint of a judgmental outsider, like a child psychologist who writes parenting books who doesn't have children or a male gynecologist. If you don't have a vagina, you just can't relate. I've been a slut, a wife, a whore, a cheater, and a gold digger, so take my advice here. Also, these aren't isolated incidents. I have had several lovers. If you keep running into the same type of man, it is you, honey, who's the problem, not him. You haven't learned from your mistakes yet. Once you begin to be approached by a higher caliber of man, you will know that you finally have learned necessary lessons, and that you aren't willing to go back to bullshit. You aren't "shawty," "red," "black," or "yella." If the motherfucker wants to talk to you, you are *miss* or *ma'am* until you tell him otherwise.

- Don't lose the respect of a green-flag man by sleeping with him too soon. The longer you wait, the better.

- Don't allow a man to stay with you if he doesn't have his own place. He shouldn't come from Mom's house to your house. He needs to stand on his own two feet first.

- Don't pick up a man to go out on a date. If he wants to see you, he will make it happen.

- Don't date a man who is unemployed or says he has his own business. Lots of drug dealers and pimps will tell you they work for themselves, and they do. But you don't want that anywhere near you! Can you find his "business" on the internet? Does he have employees? Is it legit?

- Don't sleep with him immediately, especially not on the first date. Men will pressure you, and promise you the moon in order to get sex, but after it's over, his behavior will change, and ninety percent of the time, it will be for the worst. If you are really interested in him, wait at least two months. No oral sex either. Kissing is just fine.

- Walk away from criminals, thugs, hoodlums, and anyone who lacks integrity. This goes for white collar criminals too. Just because he's in a suit doesn't mean he isn't a thug.

- Don't allow him in your home until you know where he lives, works, and who his people are. Never give your address out on a first date. Meet him at your date destination. If you do allow him over, tell someone that you are having Mr. Such and Such over, and give whoever it is as much information as possible. Women are raped and murdered in their own homes by men who they allowed in because they thought they knew them.

- SINGLE MOTHERS: Don't allow him to meet your children until you know that you are in a committed relationship that is headed toward marriage. You don't want your child becoming attached to a man who's temporary.

- Don't stay in a situation that feels wrong. Trust your gut! If it feels wrong, it is wrong.

- Don't ever chase a man who won't chase you. If he isn't calling you to ask you out, he doesn't want to. Men are that simple.

- Don't go through his phone unless you know your hands are clean. Are you hiding something too? Karma has a way of paying us back in these cases. Never ever mention your sneaky act to him.

- Don't try to change a man. He will only change if he wants to. It's impossible, so don't even waste your time.

- Don't emasculate, shout, or "go off" on him in front of others.

- Don't ever criticize these three things: his dick, his job (which equals how much money he makes), or his car.

- Don't flirt with his friends—ever.
- SINGLE MOTHERS: Never leave a boyfriend alone with children. Only do so if your children are old enough to drive a car, in which case they are old enough to call for help or defend themselves.
- Don't allow a man to cheat on you. There's no excuse! He doesn't want you.
- Don't date a married or separated man. If he is divorced, ask to see a decree, or search through public records for it.
- Don't be a stuck up, snobby, princess bitch. Just respect yourself, and he will too. If he doesn't, FUCK HIM. Move on!
- Don't tell a man how bad you've been previously treated in hopes that he won't do the same to you. This always backfires (for some reason). Even if he asks, just say it didn't work out. Don't elaborate.
- Guard your emotions. Women are ruled by their hearts, and in the dating game this fact is public enemy number one. It also makes you a mark; a target for men who are looking for weakness in you. It all boils down to how easily they can break you so they can eventually fuck you. Nothing else. Don't show them your weak spots. Build a fortress around your heart and your emotions. Men really don't give a shit about how you

feel when they meet you. All they can think about is your ass bouncing up and down on their dicks.

- Don't get drunk. Give yourself a one-drink maximum, and never leave your drink at the table while you go to the restroom. Always finish your drink before getting up, because you can never be too sure. A guy can slip anything in your drink when you're not looking. Common date rape drugs include Flunitrazepam, or Rohypnol (also known as "roofies"), Gamma Hydroxybutyric acid, or GHB (also known as liquid ecstasy), and ketamine, (also known as "Special K"), these drugs can come in a variety of forms, from pills to liquids to powders. In summary:

  o Don't accept drinks from other people.

  o Open containers yourself.

  o Keep your drink with you at all times, even when you go to the bathroom.

  o Don't share drinks.

  o Don't drink from punch bowls or other common, open containers. They may already have drugs in them.

  o If someone offers to get you a drink from a bar or at party, go with that person to order your drink. Watch the drink being poured, and then carry it yourself.

- o Don't continue to drink anything that tastes or smells strange. GHB, for instance, often has a salty taste to it.
- o Have a sober friend with you to make sure nothing happens.
- o If you realize you've left your drink unattended, pour it out.
- o If you feel drunk and haven't had any alcohol, or if the effects of the alcohol you've had to drink seem much stronger than usual, get help right away.

Chapter 5

The Dos

"I go forth alone and I stand as ten thousand."
—Maya Angelou

I know all the don'ts have probably weighed you down, and you might be thinking, "How will I ever remember it all?" Don't worry. You don't have to memorize everything; just read it a few times. The brain is phenomenal, and you are only using a small portion of it. What you see and what you read is subconsciously stored deep in your brain. When the time arises, you will unconsciously tap into that part of your brain and reject any bullshit that comes your way. If you feel it is bullshit, and you accept it anyways, you need to take a reflective moment and look in the mirror. I mean it. Look at yourself. What is it about this situation that makes you want to break all the rules?

Keep in mind that you can't change what or who he is. You can only change yourself and your surroundings. You are the key master. You can open any door you choose. Some doors are harder to close than others. Some doors have had the knobs broken off. Make sure they are doors worth opening. Project positive energy into the universe through your thoughts, actions, and prayers. You will get back what you throw out there. Project negativity and pessimism, and you will get back exactly what you've asked for.

- Do give a good man a chance, even if he isn't your physical ideal. I have been in love, and have been turned on by some of the ugliest men God ever did create. Why and how did these unattractive men capture my special attention? These men were great guys, and they were nice guys that every other woman ignored. After I went out with each of them and found out how awesome they all were, each one turned into Idris Elba for me! I was turned on by his heart, and that's what you ultimately want. Don't be mistaken, either, because your rose will soon begin to lose its bloom, and you too will hope and want someone to see the beauty that lies inside of you. That said, don't force yourself to like or love a guy simply because he's a good guy. If you simply aren't attracted to

57

him, and can never even fathom sleeping with him, then let him go. Don't lead him on. You gave it a try and you couldn't get with it. Set him free so some other woman (who just might be waiting to claw your eyes out) can have him.

- Respect yourself. People can only treat you how you let them. Presentation is everything. When a man or woman has disrespected you, let them know immediately. Being this way allows them to know who you are, and what you will and won't tolerate.

- Dress accordingly. Men love a little mystery. Dress like a lady, but keep it classy; a small amount of cleavage and just enough leg. At no time should your cleavage be so on display that he can see the beginnings of your areolas. Keep the length of your skirt tasteful. You shouldn't have to constantly be pulling your skirt down all night. Wear panties! Please, ladies, keep that cat in the cage! Reserve things like this for when you are already in an established relationship. Otherwise, you will be branded a hoe. Don't wear a club dress to a barbecue. If you are invited to church, dress the part. Wear your most modest dress, not your best club dress. Wear pantyhose and a bra, as you are being presented in the house of the Lord. Show some respect.

- Listen to everything he says carefully. Men usually say what they mean no matter how uncomfortable it makes you. Women sometimes take the rude things men say as jokes. Men are very succinct—they say what they men. Unlike women, they rarely beat around the bush.

- *Do believe him the first time if he shows you he's crazy.* In the words of Iyanla Vanzant, "When you see crazy coming, cross the street!" He is what he is, sister. There's nothing you can do for him, so the best thing you can do is for yourself, which is *leave.* If you feel your life is in danger, wait until he goes to work or to sleep, and get the hell out!

- On first dates, always meet in a well-lit public place. Always let your friends or family know where you are going and with whom. Give all the information you can about this person. Share his Facebook profile, Instagram account, and Twitter accounts with them if you have any of these things. Take a picture of his license plate, make sure you know his full name, and send both to a friend. Text your route to your friend and what places you're going to be that night. Let your friend know when you anticipate coming back, and that you'll text or call if you're going to be later than that. Remember, you don't know this guy. Who he is tonight isn't the same person you might get once alcohol is consumed. This is his representative, the person who he pretends to be on interviews and around church members. Does this sound extreme to you? That's because it is. Welcome to the real world, baby cakes. If you don't want to end up kidnapped or in a ditch, you have to safeguard yourself. Women end up missing and murdered every day under these same circumstances. Thousands of women are never heard from again until a body is washed up in a creek, or someone who is walking a dog stumbles upon a bone—which could be one of your bones, your skull, or your skeleton. No one is ever the same person who they first appear to be. Not even you.

- Social media has almost single-handedly put private investigators out of work. There have been more crimes solved than ever before because of social networks like Facebook, Instagram, and Twitter. We crave so much attention that we put our every move online. From our children's birthday parties, to our food, drug use, and even when we're sick, we post about it, and ninety percent of the time it's visible to complete strangers.

- Speak with vague optimism. If you are lonely and desperate, he doesn't need to hear you say that. Don't give away too much personal information.

- Ask him questions about who he is and what he wants out of life. Why not? No need to waste time on someone who is just looking to chill. A man who says he just wants to kick it and chill is being straight up with you. "Chilling" means fucking with no dating and no commitment. Even if he isn't a potential love interest, he might become a good friend, and you don't want negative, stagnant people in your life. You should always surround yourself with people who can bless you and have a positive influence on your life, people who can teach you new things that will make you want to further your ambitions.

- Do look him up on any public records that are available to you. Again, I know this is an extreme way to find out about someone, but you will be amazed at what information is publicly available. Men lie—a lot—and even with all this searching and high-tech-Nancy-Drew investigative work, there will still be things you won't find out about him until you catch him. I found out through public records that my then-boyfriend had been married, divorced, and had owned several different homes, and also to whom those homes were sold to. On Facebook alone I found out that he had three other women on the side, one of which he did a full maternity photo shoot with. Yeah, she was pregnant. So much can be found out even if you dig just a little bit.

- Check the FBI's Most Wanted list and the list of sexual predators available through public records. This is especially important if you have children.

- Do listen to ex-girlfriend's, ex-wives, and baby mamas. I'm not saying all these women will be telling you one hundred percent of the truth, but listen for consistencies in their stories. I have dealt with this so many times. I have felt threatened that the other woman was trying to ruin our relationship because she didn't want us to be together. That may be partly true, I'm sure, but looking back on these relationships, what I found out to be true about these men was exactly what these women were trying to tell me. Also, if your family and friends are concerned, you should be too. The people who really know and love us can smell a dog a mile away. Yes, they do need to mind their business, but you also need to listen.

- Realize that you are the prize. If you ever feel grateful to be on a date with a man, leave. He should be making you feel as like you did *him* a favor, and not the other way around. Your time is valuable, and you are valuable. He wants you, and needs what you have to offer. Yes, I am talking about your vagina. Yes, you have more to offer than sex, but in a man's mind, all he sees is sex until he falls in love with you. Until then, you are pussy, and nothing more.

- Please masturbate. It is good for you, and it will help keep your mind off the real thing. You need it to take the edge off, especially when you are trying to save yourself for that special person. Just don't overdo it.

- Do see potential, but don't let it be all you see. Potential should turn into ambition, and ambition should turn into action.

part 3

---

lessons

Chapter 6

The Art of Discretion

"When the mouth stumbles,
it is worse than the foot"
—African Proverb

We've all heard the expression "TMI" (Too Much Information), along with other overly used clichés, such as "ignorance is bliss" and "what you don't know can't hurt you." My married best friend tells me that I should be able to be honest, and tell my nonexistent husband everything, and that this honesty is the very core of what makes a relationship work and last. Blah! I love you, dear, but I just don't agree. There are some very important things you should *never* tell a man under any circumstances. Men are not our equals. They exist in a world that was created by men, and they follow strict misogynistic and chauvinistic (sometimes unknowingly) rules, and they expect us to follow those rules as well. Unfortunately, ladies, this is a man's world and we must appear to abide. Whether you agree or disagree, here are some topics you should avoid, along with reasons why. This is based off life experience, not speculation or opinion. These are real, *true* facts that were a part of my life that involve the many men who've been in it.

NEVER TALK ABOUT EX-BOYFRIENDS, BABY DADDIES, OR EX-HUSBANDS

If you're talking about him, you're not over him, and your guy will know this. Take down all pictures of your exes, throw out his sweat shirt that you love to sleep in, and don't ever mention his name in the presence of your new man—never, unless you have absolutely no choice. Men are territorial creatures, and a man likes to imagine that he's the first guy you've been with. Let the fantasy continue. Don't ruin it.

YOUR BODY COUNT

If he wants a number, give him one, but keep it under ten. There's a double standard with this rule that goes back to the days of sultans and harems. Men can sleep with as many women as they'd like, and get a big pat on the back from the world for exhibiting their "manliness." When a woman, who is as free as any man, does the same, she is not applauded. She is ridiculed and ostracized. True story—my ex-boyfriend broke up with me when I told him I'd slept with 5 men. He, on the other hand, had literally slept with hundreds of women. He told me women weren't supposed to sleep with as many men as men had slept with women. He said every time he slept with me, all he could think about were the five guys I had had sex with before him—like I wasn't thinking every time I gave him head about the hundreds of hot pockets that had slid up and down his pole. But did I judge him? No.

You can't win here, ladies, so don't try. Once you've spilled the beans about your true number you'll never be able to take it back, and the first time he's mad at you, he'll let you know how much of a slut he really thinks you are. Don't believe me? Try it for yourself. If he doesn't believe you, act offended, and I mean get really upset. Don't talk to him for a few days to let him know he's insulted you. You have to put on the best show you can in order to make the story believable.

NEVER TALK ABOUT YOUR SEXUAL HISTORY

If you've had a ménage a trois, gang bangs, mass orgies, past treated sexually transmitted diseases, or were into S&M, keep it to yourself. (Incidentally, if you have HIV or AIDS, herpes, are currently suffering from a sexually transmitted infection, or any other incurable disease that can be transmitted sexually, tell him *upfront.* Never withhold this information! Let him make the decision as to whether or not he wants to play Russian roulette with his life. The decision is not yours alone. Don't be afraid to tell a man what's really going on, because you might be surprised what they say. I have an uncle whose girlfriend is HIV positive, and he's negative, so don't be afraid that someone won't love you because of your diagnosis.)

If he's interested in those things, just let him know you're willing to try whatever he likes. A man likes to think he's acquired a lady that he can train into a freak. Don't readily volunteer this information! If he likes to role play, being spanked, etc., let him tell you, and then you can follow through with it. Don't go in like you've been doing it for years either, or he'll suspect you've lied to him. Then the wheels in his little brain will never stop turning! If your oral sex skills can put Super Head to shame, don't show him that initially. Do it just good enough to where he thinks you have the potential to grow. This is not lying or being deceptive. Some things a lady should always keep to herself.

NEVER TELL A MAN YOU HATE YOUR BODY

If you're out of shape, fat, or have no shape at all, never tell a man this. A man wants to know that he is with a confident, self-loving woman. He doesn't want to be your self-esteem coach. High confidence and self-esteem is sexy, and even if you aren't the model type, he'll believe you are because you exude confidence. Whining about your love handles and cellulite will only draw more attention to them. Complaining is very unattractive! If you don't like what you see in the mirror, then change it! Don't expect him to love a body that you hate.

DON'T DISCUSS YOUR FINANCES

Whether you're ballin' or barely dribblin', it's no one's business except your own. Don't go whining about how you need money for stupid shit like clothes, purses, shoes, hair, or nails. You'll instantly be deemed a gold-digging tramp. Trust me, if a man wants to help you with your bills, you won't have to ask for it. He'll know if you need the help. Stop putting your stilettos in your mouth, and instead learn how to shut the fuck up. Don't parade around like you don't need any man. Everyone needs help sometimes, and if you're strutting around like Oprah, you'll never get a dime out of his ass! Furthermore, a man likes to be needed, even though he might not say it out loud. He wants to be the breadwinner. So if your salary makes his look like a stipend, you might want to keep that information to yourself. If ever the proverbial rainy day rears its ugly head, then you can just tell him you've been "saving for us." He'll be happy he got with such a frugal and smart woman. Let a man be a man, because they need that.

NEVER CONFESS TO CHEATING

Here's that double standard again, ladies. A man will never trust you again once you admit to cheating. His entire perception of you will change forever. I don't care if it happened years ago before you all first met. Never tell him. These are the secrets that should go to your grave! I think it's because women have these nurturing, motherly instincts that allow us to forgive. In the back of my mind, I always believe that a man cheating is an inevitability that I, as a grown woman, just have to face. I can forgive him because I know men are stupid. A man will not forgive you, because you're a woman, and you "should know better and have more respect for yourself." This is how a man thinks. Why volunteer information that he will never find out? You *will* find out about his infidelities, and he doesn't need to admit it. A man can run a country, save it from famine and despair, but can't seem to figure out how to have a discreet affair. Never tell him.

YOUR FRIENDS ARE WHORES

You are who you hang with, so shut the fuck up about Cheryl cheating on her boyfriend every weekend, or Tina who's sleeping with her boss. Don't tell their business to your man! Once he finds out how they really are, you'll never have a peaceful girl's night out again. Let your man think that your girls are perfect ladies. Don't ever think that you can tell your man these things, because he will never want to be around Cheryl or Tina. Parties, weddings, and get-togethers happen. The main common ingredient at these festive occasions is alcohol. Once the shot glasses start flipping, his mouth will get to slipping! You could easily find yourself single and friendless by the end of the night.

YOU HATE HIS MOTHER

Last, but certainly not least, never let him know that you despise the dragon lady otherwise known as his mother. Men hold their mothers on high pedestals, and their mothers can do no wrong. In a man's eyes, the last time his mother had sex was to create his ass. She is a perfect angel, and she is the epitome of what a woman should be. If you want to be with him long term, learn to love the old witch, and never voice your grievances about her, unless you are married and she is driving a wedge between you two.

Chapter 7

The Man You Want

"We are becoming the men
we wanted to marry."
-Gloria Steinman

"I've been divorced for a few years, but I keep running into brothers with no car, no job, and no money, guys who want to be players with hefty criminal background histories. If I had so many cons against me, then I would want to focus on getting myself together so that I can bring something to the table. Where are the single men that have jobs, a car, and no drama? No one is perfect, and I'm willing to accept a few things but I can't do the 'no job' thing."

—Laura, 31, Houston, Texas

How many times have we heard this before? It's like beating a dead horse! Ever since I was a little girl, it's been drilled into me that when choosing a man, he must have three important things: a job, which equals money, a car, which equals transportation, and a house he *owns*. If he didn't have those things he didn't have me. I honestly don't ever recall abiding by those rules, and that might be why I am single.

It might be why you are single.

The rules taught to us aren't being followed, because we aren't enforcing them. We date men with no jobs, no cars, no homes, and no real futures. Since most of us accept this nonsense from men, it has now seeped into their brains that this type of behavior is acceptable, because we accept them regardless. Sound about right? If we actually did what we were taught, and we only picked partners who had those three qualities, then all men who want women would strive to have jobs, cars, houses, and *no* drama in their lives. But since we have shown them that we will accept them without these things, bringing nothing to the table, he has no incentive to go out and get them.

This type of man is lazy, spoiled, and self-centered, and he will never give you what you need. He has no value for women unless it is for them to cater to him. He has no respect for women. He's never met a man who does. If he has met a man who respects, honors, and loves women, he will, in his homophobic fright, call him a bitch. He's dependent on you for the entire relationship, and will constantly remind you that he was this way when you met him, so why are you trying to change him now?

The truth is, he should want to change himself, but he has no need or want to feed himself when is being spoon fed. He will also tell you that he can't find a job due to his jail record. That's bullshit. You fell for it. We all have. If illegal Mexicans who don't even speak English can post up at Home Depot at 5 a.m. every morning, he can too. He has had all the opportunities everyone else has had who's been born in this country, yet he chooses to find ways to scheme, plot, hustle, steal, sell drugs, and live off the government. He didn't have a strong father figure, and neither did his father. His lack of manhood is sadly an inherited trait. He feels that he's God's gift to you because there aren't enough brothers to go around, and you're lucky to have found him.

My grandmother Eunice would ask me questions like, "He don't beat you, right? He's not on that crack rock, right? Well, then that's a *good* man!"

Excuse me while I go vomit. Sorry. I'm back. Only a few men are smart enough to have actually acquired the assets that give us the security we need in order to live comfortable lives. Only a few men have because there are truly only a few who actually exist, and they have monopolized the dating market. They know that they're a commodity for any lucky lady. He doesn't have to compete with other men that make more money or have bigger houses because they are so few and far in between. This type of man knows that he has his pick of the lot. He had a father, and knows what is expected of men. He's never been to jail for more than a traffic ticket. He's well-educated, a member of a fraternity, graduated from the best schools, wears overpriced yuppie garb, and is always in fashion. He owns more tailored suits than jeans in his wardrobe. He will out-dress you, and can tell you what designer, if any, you're wearing. He is critical, overbearing, and chauvinistic, but you can take him anywhere. He can speak in polite conversation, and discuss politics and world views with ease. When he enters the room he has the smoothest walk, and all women sit up straight when comes through the door. You are proud to present him to your family.

But he has no need to settle down when there are so many willing victims ready to be saved. Mr. Successful is the hardest man to tame. If you play love games with him to secure his fidelity, he won't mind. He won't mind, because he won't care. He's off seeing what new adventure he and his Brooks Brother's suit can get into today. He will only succumb to commitment and marriage when he is ready and has exhausted all other options. For Mr. Successful, this is usually around the age of 38 years old, when he feels like he's too old to be the nearly 40-year-old dude at the bar. It no longer looks cool—it looks sad.

He will only choose a woman who is of the same caliber as he—a line sister, college ex-girlfriend, etc. Someone who his family thinks is of the right breeding, has the right education, and is submissive to his authority. This man only commits so that he can have a family and create a legacy, just like the rest of his buddies. It will have nothing to do with his undying passion for you. This type of man commonly cheats throughout his entire marriage, but out of a sense of duty, he will never leave his wife.

Lastly, there's the man we have known about all along, Mr. Nice Guy, the guy you dumped who had the Basic Three. He's not an Ivy League scholar, but may go to a technical institute, or have received a vocational degree in something where he gets his hands dirty. He's a man's man. He is a "jack of all trades." He can fix the hole in the roof and put a new engine in your car all in the same day. He's respected by his friends, loves his mother and sisters, and to top it all off, he treats you like the Goddess Isis, and hangs on your every word.

He loves women, because women raised him, and he will kill the man who disrespects his family. He's met his father before, but shows no respect for a man who doesn't take care of family. He takes care of kids that came from your previous relationship, and he doesn't judge you. He will raise your son to be a man and he will love him, all because he loves you. Mr. Nice Guy is mediocre at best.

He will never be overly ambitious, and he is content with being middle class, watching football, and having barbeques on Sunday with his wife and kids. He's just happy to have you around. He is practical. He will never take you for granted, and will take on two or three menial jobs just to make you happy. You didn't want him because of some small imperfection that could have easily been looked over, but you just needed to find an excuse to get his boring ass out of your face.

Let's be honest, shall we? Let's see why you didn't choose Mr. Right. He's unattractive, fat, balding, has a small penis, and you're embarrassed to bring him around your friends. You know he will "never" fulfill you sexually, which will lead to cheating, and you're not that kind of woman. He's boring, and you hate routine. You don't want to settle, and he does! He lacks ambition and drive, and he has a fear of success. So what do you do? This bland, unattractive man doesn't look, act, or speak like Mr. Successful, who, by the way, favors Boris Kodjoe. Nope, Mr. Nice Guy, also known as Mr. Right, looks like Forest Whitaker, but he's kind, affectionate, and he listens. If you're tired of the hunt for Mr. Perfect, you can stop the chase now. He doesn't exist.

Women are healers! We can't help it when someone needs help. We want to give them a Band-Aid, tell them they're not alone, and send them on their way. We can't change anyone or anything. It's not in our control to do such things. You can't turn a street dog into a prize-winning horse. Remember this: We can only be treated how we let people treat us.

part 4

---

dating

Chapter 8

A Manual for the Single Mother

"A mother's love for her child is like nothing else in the world. It knows no law, no pity, it dares all things and crushes down remorselessly all that stands in its path."
—Agatha Christie

The previous chapters of this book have touched on dating when you have children and what to watch out for. This section is for mothers, expectant single mothers, and women who just want to get a better understanding of single motherhood. I applaud you childless ladies who read this chapter. You have single mother girlfriends who you just can't seem to understand. Your girlfriend has changed. She can't really hang anymore, she spells out curse words, and is tired by 9 p.m. Your friend is a mommy now, and she'll never be the same again. Congratulations for taking the time out to find understanding outside of your own point of view. This is a sign of maturity. You are the link that binds our sisterhood. Who knows, maybe you'll be the next one holding the sippy cup?

This is probably the most difficult, widely divided section of this book. When we talk about our kids, we become sensitive, defensive, and emotional. We don't like anyone telling us what to do with our kids, or who we should and shouldn't bring around them. When we are in love, like, lust, or lonely, we are also temporarily blind, deaf, and dumb as fuck. This is why I decided to start off a with a very clear-cut section that includes some of the most common questions and answers.

Q: How soon should I introduce my children to my boyfriend?

A: Some say immediately, but I disagree. Others say after you have both fully committed to one another, which I'm mostly, but not totally, against. In my opinion, you should introduce him only once he proposes, and then that year of engagement can be used for him to get to know the children.

In a recent survey of 28 anonymous male respondents, 72% of men said they'd prefer to meet the child within 6 months after he's established the seriousness of the relationship.

Q: Should I allow my boyfriend to sleep over while my kids are asleep?

A: No. You may get away with sneaking him out the door a few times before 7 a.m. rolls around, but eventually they'll burst in the room and no mommy wants to have to explain the naked man in her bed.

Q: What should my children address my boyfriend as?

A: No first names. He is Mr. Whoever until you become Mrs. Whoever. Children should respect adults. He isn't "Daddy" yet. He has to earn that title by solidifying the relationship. By keeping the title in effect, it lets the children know that he isn't personally a part of their lives yet. This can be a good thing, as it will allow for the children to not become attached to someone who won't be there tomorrow.

Q: Should I allow the father of my children to meet my boyfriend?

A: Again, your boyfriend shouldn't be allowed to meet the children until he has proposed or until you have dated long enough to know that the relationship is headed toward marriage. This does not include you just having a feeling he'll marry you. This means that a conversation has taken place between the two of you where you're both in agreement on the trajectory of this relationship. Once you have allowed him to meet your kids, then he can meet your ex. A grown responsible man who cares about his children will jump at the opportunity to meet the man who will essentially be his replacement. If your current man isn't serious about you, he won't be willing to meet the ex. If he is a fraud, he knows that another man will sniff this out quicker than a blood hound, and he will strongly be against meeting him. If your ex is not in the picture, have your boyfriend meet a close male relative or friend whom you trust. Don't bring anyone around that you have slept with, however, as his motives might be questionable.

Q: How soon should I sleep with a man I'm interested in?

A: This goes across the board, whether you're a single mom or a single lady, don't sleep with any man for at least sixty to ninety days after you all have seriously started dating. Test how serious he is about you. Go as long as you can! Most guys who are out to use and abuse, will give up after two fuck-less dates! You'll be able to easily weed out the douchebags. I don't care what he says. Don't give in too early. Remember men are well versed on what to say to get a woman naked. Once he gets what he wants, he will be gone with no interest in seeing you again. Men are motivated by very few things: sex, money, food, and sports. In that order. Did you notice love and commitment wasn't on that list? If he does call you again, know that you are just booty. He'll never commit to you, so please don't get upset with him after you have been fucking for six months and he still won't commit. You opened this door, and you have the power over what type of relationship you get, and it lies right between your legs. Masturbating and keeping busy is the easiest way to stay focused from not having sex with the man you really want to be with. Kissing and touching is fine, but know your limit! It will be a daunting task, but if you can succeed at withholding the puss from him, it'll pay off in the end. You'll find out one of two things: he'll either want to commit to you or he won't.

In a recent survey of 28 anonymous male respondents, 43% stated it depended on the woman as to whether or not they'd still respect her if she slept with them on the first date, while 36% stated they might consider calling her again.

SPONTANEITY AND RESPONSIBILITY FOR THE SINGLE MOTHER

You are no longer the carefree girl with the wind in her hair who can make plans for a weeklong trip to Mexico in an hour. You are a mother now; you have the major responsibility of another person's human life. You simply can't drop what you are doing and leave. I'm sorry, but you can't. You don't have the life that your married girlfriend has. She has a husband, hopefully supportive, who allows her to have fun occasionally while he holds down the fort. Not you, sister, there's only you. When a guy asks you out on a date for that same day, don't immediately say yes because you're dying to get out of the house. Don't seem desperate, even if you are. Let him know that you are a single mother, and that you will always need twenty-four to forty-eight hours' notice if he wants to take you out. You have to make arrangements and get proper sitters for your children. A real man will respect you for this. This is a true sign that you are a good mother that you won't drop your kids off with granny the minute someone asks you out. Unfortunately, spontaneity is not an option for single moms. Don't blame this on your children either. They didn't ask to be here. Grow up and deal with your womanhood. I would've given up spontaneity years ago if I knew how happy my daughter would make me.

SHOW OFF

We all love to show people pictures of our kids. They are our pride and joy! Our Facebook timelines are flooded with back-to-school pictures, Easter-egg hunts, and family Christmas photos. Don't show the guy you are dating pictures of your kids or where they attend school; name and ages should be enough. Make up an excuse, like "I just cleaned out my phone." If he persists, let him know that you don't feel comfortable giving out such personal information about your children. If he can't understand that, drop his ass. Pedophilia is a real disease, and sometimes a man will date you to get to your child.

Pedophiles, like serial killers and psychopaths, look like regular people. Don't think that because he's so nice that you can guarantee he would never do such a thing. We all wear masks every day, and no one is ever who they appear to be. Never base your gut feelings off appearances. Appearances tell us nothing. As a single mother, you're ripe game for a manipulator. The fact that you have no man in the house makes you a target for predators. You are easy game. A predator, user, or a psychopath realizes that there is something missing from your life, something you want more than anything—a responsible father figure for your children. He will try to intentionally plug himself into the parenting equation. He will seem genuinely concerned about your little one. Let him know where you stand upfront on this. Protecting your kids is your number one concern as a mother. Yes, he's fine, and has this and that, but how do you feel about him? Trust your gut instincts. If it doesn't feel right, get rid of him.

BABY SITTING

Never allow a boyfriend to take care of your kids while you are away. He should never be an option. If there's no one else around, change your plans or take them with you. Unless they are old enough to drive, I wouldn't advise this, especially young babies, newborns, and toddlers who are the most trusting and most defenseless creatures on God's planet. I don't want this to come off as if no man is to be trusted, but when it comes to your children, no precaution is ever too much. Most pedophiles look for opportunities to be alone with your child, or will offer themselves up as sitters. He appears to be helpful and friendly, and the kids love him. Pedophiles instill fear in a child in exchange for their silence. Take a moment and think about the many cases you've heard on the news and seen on your Facebook timeline about child molestation and murder at the hands of a boyfriend or stepfather. The cases are innumerable and tragic. Be on your guard at all times. I can't stress this enough.

Chapter 9

Casual Sex

"Sex: The thing the takes up the least amount of time, and causes the most amount of trouble."
—John Barrymore

When I was a younger and more arrogant woman, I believed that I could sleep with men and easily dispose of them, as they did to me after they had slept with me. I thought that I could act like a man and still be a woman. I was hurt, and I wanted to hurt or not have any emotions, just as they had had no emotions after sleeping with me—not once, but several times. As I got older and the list of my sexual partners grew, I realized that I couldn't have casual sex and not become emotionally tied. I am not a man, and I never will be. Women are not wired the same way as men. Women equate sex with love, and men equate sex with sex. Men don't put the two together. As a matter of fact, men usually marry a woman with whom they have had little to no sexual experience with. Contrary to what you might think men want, when men look to enter into a committed relationship or marriage, they look for qualities such as a loyalty, intelligence, whether she has a good education, and if she'd be a good mother. Being beautiful and great in the sack are at the bottom of the list. Hell, those two things barely even make the list.

In a recent survey of anonymous males, thirty percent stated that when looking for a bride or life partner, intelligence and education were number one on their list, while twenty-six percent stated that loyalty was the one thing they looked for. They don't marry or commit to the girl who gives up the prize too soon or who doesn't exhibit moral boundaries. Most women aren't capable of having casual sex repeatedly with the same man and not catching feelings. It is impossible. Say what you want, but you will think about this man every waking hour, and eventually you will wonder why he hasn't committed to you, or why he only calls you after midnight to come chill.

Just because a man you are screwing becomes jealous of the idea of you with another man, doesn't mean he loves you. Men are jealous and territorial by nature. Just like a dog, they mark their territory and they will bare teeth when another dog pisses on their tree. It has nothing to do with love. It's all territory, and men don't like to share. They can have you, and many other women as well, but you better not have anyone else. Women think that this means he loves you. It doesn't. Understand and know who you are as a woman. Men are givers and women are receivers. Don't think you are being this super cool, she-man bitch who has no emotions. At the end of all casual sex, remember this, you are the one getting fucked, not him. If you feel you can have casual sex and have no emotions involved, go ahead, but stay protected. Protect your body and your heart.

I don't recommend sleeping with the same man more than twice, as you are sure to get emotionally involved. Hit it and quit it. Twice is all your female hormones will allow before you give in, your emotions creep in, and you start envisioning a wedding and what your kids will look like with this guy. Don't be ashamed; it's how we are. If you have to have sex to stay afloat or to stay motivated, but don't really have time for a relationship and all that one entails, become a serial dater. You'll have to look at men like a can of nuts. If you just choose peanuts, that's all you'll want, and you'll become hooked on one man, who, like you, came into this with the agreement that it would be nothing more than casual sex. Now you have gotten emotional. But if you pick up a can of mixed nuts, you'll have a variety to choose from and sleep with. Date and sleep with different men, just please *always wear condoms AND use birth control.* I don't care how good the dick is! Or how often you've slept with him. You are not committed to him, and you are *not* the only woman he is screwing.

When women sleep with one man, they close off the rest of the dating pool and put all their energy into one man who might not even be all that interested in them. This is how we get our female feelings hurt, putting all our eggs in one basket. Keep these liaisons a secret. Only tell one close friend (in the event that you come up missing as previously discussed). Also, keep your personal life private and skip the pillow talk! He is just a piece of meat that you need to get off on for a little while. He doesn't need to know what your favorite color is or what your life goals are. Believe me, he doesn't care, and neither should you if you want this casual sex thing to really work. It is hard for a woman to forget her heart, but seriously, leave her ass at home.

Chapter 10

Social Media Accounts

"Women are roses, whose fair flower being once displayed, doth fall that very hour."
-William Shakespeare

CLEAN UP YOUR SOCIAL MEDIA ACCOUNTS

What do you want—attention, a new career, a husband, or a boyfriend? In our society, we are judged for what appears on our social media accounts. Let's face it; the vast majority of those of us who are considered millennials (or Generation Y) live online. We all know the supposedly slutty girl who posts the tits and ass pictures. Is a woman who shows all of her body on social media a slut? If she gets one hundred likes from thirsty guys telling her she's perfect, is she a slut? How about the mother who posts nude photos of herself and the newborn suckling at her breast? Is she also a slut? Is there a difference in one nude woman from another? One might be considered art, while the other is considered trash.

I created a book for my daughter that shows my journey through pregnancy, from delivery to age one, and then finishing at two years old. Some people considered it be a beautiful keepsake, while others have considered it risqué and almost lewd. My point in saying this to you is that we all are judged harshly on what is displayed on social media. Even the nude artistic mom is looking for likes. What are you looking for? What is your reason for displaying your body to strange men who will only make you empty promises? Men are enticed by what they see. Every man has seen you. It will not be hard to find a man, but it will be hard to find a good man. Social media will be the death of our humanity. Here are a few tips on surviving in Death Valley.

- Do not post any booty or breast shots.
- Do not use stupid sign-in names.
- Delete all pictures of clubbing, children, ex-husbands/boyfriends, drug use (even hookah smoking), and obscene and vulgar videos (even if they're funny). Remember, men want a lady or at least the appearance there of.
- Do not post any vulgar nudity whatsoever. Nursing your kids and/or artistic nudity is

acceptable. Society is still starkly split on the porn vs. art debate, so be careful.

- Make sure your grammar and spelling are correct when making posts. If you write like an idiot, you'll find an idiot who speaks your language.
- Don't check in anywhere. You think this is harmless? Don't be so naïve. You are beautiful, and you are being watched.
- Be careful of who tags you, and watch out for scandalous pictures. Facebook has a setting that lets you approve or disapprove who tags you. Use it!

part 5

spirit & mind

Chapter 11

Your Spiritual Self

"You don't have a soul; you are a soul.
You have a body."
—C.S. Lewis

Reality has become a lie, and my dreams are the only things that are real to me, that are tangible and worth holding on to. Once you understand and know that you are more than just flesh, then, and only then, will you begin to see yourself as the soul you are; a living, invincible non-physical being incapable of perishing. Nothing that has lived can ever really die. Throughout my anguish, there have been many teachers that have helped bring me along my spiritual journey, most of whom I admire dearly: Oprah, Les Brown, Iyanla Vanzant, Bea Richardson, Nina Simone, Maya Angelou, Cicely Tyson, Malcolm X, Barack and Michelle Obama, Will and Jada

Smith, Tupac Shakur, Socrates, Langston Hughes, and most importantly, my mother and grandmother. Check out Super Soul Sundays on OWN. It's my church on Sunday mornings. It offers reflection, meditation, and insightful interviews from world spiritual leaders.

You don't have to be a devout anything to worship God, or whatever you want to call him or her. Some call this spiritual presence the universe, while others call it Allah, Buddha, Krishna, or Jesus. As long as you are working on being a more in-tune version of yourself every day, then you have won half the battle. You can't and won't be in a successful relationship until you first are in love with yourself. Find a quiet place of reflection every day, if only for fifteen minutes, and, surrounded in tranquility, close your eyes, breathe, and envision the real life you want to live and how you will get there. Your soul is just like a plant; it must be watered every day to keep it alive. Many people find solace in prayers and meditation. Writing is also a way of getting out what couldn't be said. Working on your dreams every day will keep you happy, motivated, and full of ambition.

Ambition and motivation are like drugs for me. Once I get it, I can't get enough of it. I have to have more! Becoming a self-starting, self-motivating, and full-of-ambition woman will attract the same type of man to you. The energy that you pass off into the world will attract the same type of mate. Your aura is a magnet.

If you are projecting positivity, good vibes, and energy, you will attract people to you who have the same type of energy. This is what you want. Keep your mind positive and optimistic about the future at all times. Ever notice that when you say you're having a bad day that it just seems to get worse from that point on? You just told the universe that you want to have a bad day, and that is what it gave you. We are our thoughts. Practice speaking life, love, abundance, and gratitude every day, even in the face of failure, disappointment, and tragedy. This is not easy to do, but you must begin to at least practice it. You are the only one who can give you the life you want and deserve, not a man, but *you*. You are the most important relationship you'll ever be in.

Chapter 12

Taken

"And those who were seen dancing,
were thought to be insane by those
who couldn't hear the music."
—Freidrich Nietzsche

What does it mean to be swept off your feet? What does it feel like when love has taken over all your logical reasoning? Is this feeling ever really real? It feels real, doesn't it? It's as real as fire burning your flesh. And you probably wouldn't mind the burn if you could just keep that feeling, the sweet euphoric aftermath of love that seems to die as quickly as it is born. False love is a still birth. Have you been taken? Can you think of nothing else but him? Why hasn't he called? Is he thinking of me? Does he still love me? What did I do wrong? Should I call him?

I cannot stop you from being taken, and no one can. I can only help you acknowledge your captivity, for once you have been taken over, there's nothing that can be done for you. To be taken is to be in the terminal stages of cancer, and to have only just found out yesterday. You'll have to die to get out of it. But once you have passed over, you know what it is to suffer, and you'll never want to return. You'll make better choices. You'll still cry from time to time when no one is looking. Sometimes you'll cry all day internally, and no one will see the weeping soul behind your smiling eyes. The only way you can break free from this hold is if you really want to.

You hold the keys to your own cage. You can leave anytime you want to, if you really want to leave. No one will be able to convince you to leave. Make a list. Draw a T-shape down the middle of a paper and write down the pros and the cons of the relationship. If the cons outweigh the pros, get the fuck out of there. No one is perfect, but, damn, you don't need a build-a-bear man either. You don't have time for that shit. You have your own problems that you haven't dealt with yet, not to mention your personal goals and projects that are continually being pushed back because you're dealing with a mental patient.

Let me say something to you for a few seconds like I know you. Sometimes the dick is so good and the man is so bad, that we will make up any excuse just so we can keep getting that long stroke. And let's face it— the dudes with the best dick are some of the biggest assholes. They know they have good dick, and they know that it is hard to come by. Pun intended. They are what my good girlfriend Dinelle calls "Community Dick" (CD). They belong to everyone. It is very easy to become "taken" by Community Dick. Don't be a victim. If you must hit it, then hit it once, and move on. Believe me, you don't want to end up on World Star, fighting with different women over CD, because you foolishly thought that you were the only one he was sleeping with.

Chapter 13

The Three You's—
Mind, Heart, and Pussy

"The universe and I exist together,
and all things and I are one."
—Chuang Tzu

There is this common perception that men and their penises share two different identities, that the penis has a brain of its own and it never follows the instructions of the brain on its shoulders. Well let me tell you, sister. This concept also applies to you. Men aren't the only ones who can have excuses for immoral sexual decisions. There's a slight difference when it comes to women who men don't include in their decision making. We include our heart in everything we do. This must stop. There are three different women who live inside you: Keisha, Sheila, and Pam. I'm kidding, but seriously, you can name them anything you want, but they are no less existent.

Let's say Keisha symbolizes your mind—smart, focused and determined. Keisha has a plan for the future, goals she'd like to accomplish, and every day she is working toward those goals. Keisha is organized, a people person, career driven, and has no time for anything that isn't directly propelling her financially or successfully. Her clothes are sharp and expensive, if not all designer or couture. Keisha is arrogant, self-centered, and at times overly confident. She only dates men that are the male versions of her. She never sleeps with a man on a first date, and will make him wait as long as she deems possible in order to secure his fidelity. Keisha keeps Sheila locked away inside a cage in her basement, and feeds her bread and water once a week. Pam is her secret home girl who none of her other friends know about. Keisha is afraid of Pam, and doesn't have the nerve to lock her away with Sheila. Pam would break out, and then everyone would know that she had put her away. Then what would everyone think?

Sheila is your heart. She is gentle, kind, and soft. She volunteers at hospices, shelters, and clinics. She wants to save the world. She is a church-goer and a devout Christian. She knows every scripture, and updates her Facebook profile with daily affirmations. She is a down-home girl who you can call if you need help, a baby sitter, or a loan. She's reliable, and always places herself second. Sheila usually gets with men who use her or treat her as a door mat. She can't understand why she can't find a good man after all she does for them. Sheila doesn't care about expensive clothing, as long as she looks nice and is clean. Sheila never has an attitude, and she is very sensitive. She is trust worthy and almost gullible. Sheila will make time for you while neglecting her own responsibilities. Sheila pretends she isn't friends with Pam, and will deny her when Jesus comes back. Sheila is terrified of Keisha, but she is grateful that someone like Keisha even speaks to her—even if she does lock her up in cage every evening.

Pam is your pussy. Pam is a gangster. She doesn't give a fuck about Keisha or Sheila. As a matter of fact, she can't stand those two bitches who keep fucking up and interfering in her plans. Pam has a one-track mind. When Pam sees dick, she takes dick and leaves dick. Keisha only calls her anonymously, because she doesn't want Pam to ruin her image, damage her billboards, and crumble her business cards. But she needs Pam like she needs air. Pam doesn't like being taken for granted, or being hidden away. Pam is plotting against Keisha in her workplace. The new guy, ten years Keisha's junior, Pam will have him for lunch and pretend it never happened. She wants what she wants and is not ashamed of who she is. But she is ashamed of Sheila. Stupid, weak Sheila. Pam has a plan. Sheila must go, and Keisha agrees that no one will miss Sheila. They are correct; no one misses Sheila except Keisha and Pam. They mourn and lament Sheila's absence, but there's no way of bringing back the dead.

Now Keisha and Pam are one, best friends, feathers flocked together in hate and secrets kept. They've decided to move in together. The heat never works, and the wood refuses to burn in the fireplace. Their posh gray architecturally modern home is cold, icy even. Pam and Keisha bicker and fight constantly. Keisha can't even secure a boyfriend these days, and Pam is so desperate that she scares men away. They are fed up and have no one left to blame. They lock up their stone palace, and stay inside the wintry fortress of bitterness and forbid visitors. Pam dies first, and Keisha remains, alone with only her pride and a once-promising future.

Who has won the battle in your life? And who remains? Has Pam, Keisha, or Sheila taken over in your life? Or have you found a way to balance these three ladies in perfect harmony? It's okay if one of them is winning and the other two are losing. Guess what? All three of them need therapy. If there is no enemy within, no outside force can defeat you.

Epilogue

"Slowly, surely, I walk away from…. that old desperate and dazed love…. caught up in the maze of love, the crazy craze of love, thought it was good, thought it was real, thought it was, but it wasn't love."
—Jill Scott

At the end of the day, no one can tell you what is best for you. We all know the right decision to make, what to do, and how to do it—inherently. The only thing that stops us is our lack of control, our non-existent will power to say *no*. No, I will not allow myself to be made a fool of again and again. No, I will not take back a man who abused, cheated on me, and made me fearful for my life. No, I will not allow myself to be taken advantage of, ignored, and used.

No matter what you have been through, you are alive to read this book, and that means one thing: You are a survivor. There isn't one woman who doesn't have a story to tell of broken hearts and dreams that have turned into nightmares. Some of you are still in the nightmare, and you don't know how to wake up. Seek help if you want to awaken. Talk to a friend who can help you get out. Not all of us are strong enough to leave a bad situation on our own. We might need the hand of a friend to help guide us out.

In the end, there are no rules and there are no trophies, only battlefields left with the scattered dead of rotting hearts and pride broken over rocks. No one can even remember why it seemed so necessary to go this far, to fight this hard, only to be left empty handed. In the game of love, there are no winners. Maybe it's because it's not to be played as a game. It is too dangerous, too fatal, and it can kill quicker than cancer. It's always "us against them." We have to, as mature human beings, start to look at love and relationships on equal footing.

For so long, I've hated being a woman. The idea of womanhood, for me, was a weakness, and I abhor anything that is weak. To me, women always received the very least of everything. Women always had to just take it. Whatever that "it" is—a cheating husband, a job that pays you less than your male colleague, the hard decision to terminate a pregnancy so that society won't judge you for becoming a single mother but now you are judged as a murderer—TAKE IT!

I used to be so envious of men and their supposed freedoms. Then I realized that they are the real prisoners. They are bound by strict, rigid, societal structures that don't allow for much self-expression or sentimentality. Outside of being applauded for their sexual prowess and promiscuity, there's not much more that men are allowed to get away with. A man must be a man, no exceptions, or he is deemed by his peers as weak, soft, or even gay, which can segregate him into becoming a social pariah. Even gay men are still men, and they handle their business!

I left an abusive boyfriend in Tennessee who'd stick his dick in a wet hole if it was warm. When I gave the numerous reasons why I wanted to leave, I was told I hadn't grown up yet and that *all men cheated.*

An older girlfriend asked, "Are you going to leave every man who cheats on you?" Therein lies the problem with women. Yes, I should leave a man who sleeps around on me. Why is that even a question? When we forgive bad behavior, we give license for it to prevail. Women have forgiven bad male behavior since the beginning of time. Mainly, we gave this forgiveness because it was practical. A woman had no choice but to forgive her husband. What else was she to do in an era when women couldn't work, earn their own money, or own their own properties? This prejudice towards females was intentionally set up to make women solely dependent on their husbands. God forbid you were over twenty-five years old and still unwed with nothing but spinsterhood to look forward to.

In our modern society, there's no excuse any longer to forgive a man just so you can be comfortable, unless you want to live a dependent life. Always yearn to and choose to be your own woman. It was only a few years ago, that I realized the real power that I possessed as a woman. I wasn't weak, and I didn't have to "take" anything. These are the thoughts of a fearless and powerful woman! We women have all the cards in our hands. Men do everything they do in life so that they can get the attention of women. They want the highest paid careers, the most expensive clothes and cars, just to win the affections of women. Remember this: You'll never have to go out of your way to impress a man who wants you. Once his mind is made up, the only person that can stop him is you.

Your chest is heavy, and there's this knot you can't seem to swallow down. You are sick to your stomach, and there's nothing you can take besides whiskey that'll make the pain subside. You went to sleep last night with a runny nose and tears in your eyes, and now, when you look in the mirror, your face is swollen from crying all night long. You even cried in your sleep. You feel like you will never get over this point. You feel like you will never forget him, and your life will never be the same. You can't even begin to understand what your friends are telling you, that this is temporary because what you've lost you thought was so permanent.

Your heart is broken.

It'll be a long, hard, and filthy road, but you will make it through, muddy boots and all.

About the Author

A single mother from Houston, Texas, Kimberly Michelle is a full-time English literature student. A writer with a flair for the raw truth and a self-described hopeless romantic, she aims to motivate women everywhere to become well-versed on all issues concerning women and misogynistic world views.

References

"Slut." Merriam-Webster.com. Merriam-Webster,n.d. Web. 3 Jan. 2016.

What Men Want, Jackson, K. (2015). Survey Monkey. Retrieved from http://www.surveymonkey.com

(2014). How Can I protect myself from becoming a victim? Retrieved from http://www.womenshealth.gov

Made in the USA
Middletown, DE
21 April 2018